letters to my daughter

Vinita Rk

Presentation by *BookLeaf Publishing*

Web: www.bookleafpub.com

E-mail: info@bookleafpub.com

ISBN: 9789363312098

First edition 2024

This book is for, to and because of Kayra, my daughter, my inspiration and my motivation.

I love you, more than you will ever know.

Mumma, I am okay..

Teaching you to ride a bike,

Was such a humbling experience,

"Mumma, don't be so scared"—you tell me, as you
climb on the bike without training wheels

"Mumma, I am not that hurt"—you assure me, as
you fall and get up to restart the journey again

"Mumma, I can do it"—you promise me with big,
solemn eyes that always melt my heart

As a Mumma, I am so weak when it comes to you,
my love

You are my strength

And your words, give me the courage

You were riding the bike that day, my girl

But, I was the one terrified

I saw you ride, wind flapping your dark hair

Your pink bike growing distant as you ride

And,

I let you go that day,

As I will let you go everyday,

To be young and free

Like you said, "Mumma, I will be okay..."

My Daughter, My Teacher

She may not be an adult
But
She taught me to put someone else above me
She taught me to come up with creatively sneaky
recipes and games that we play endlessly
She taught me to survive on a few hours of sleep
yet, wake up energetic for her all days of the year

More than anything,
She taught me to love endlessly
And, be thankful for the smallest moments in life
every single day

And, as she grows,
She continues to teach me something new every
single day

My daughter, My teacher

For the Child In You

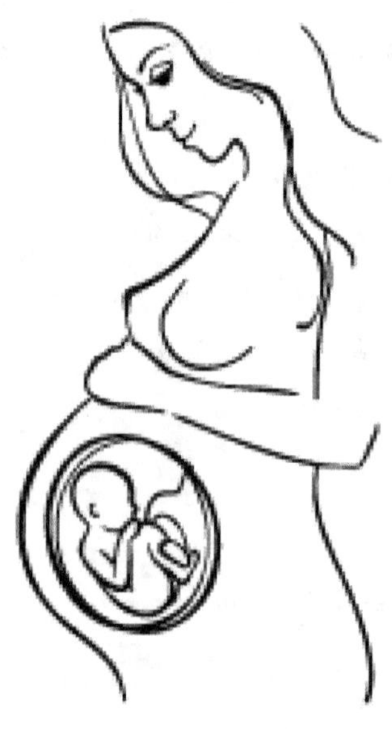

All it takes is 18 years,
18 summers
And
18 winters
For,
Tiny fingers that clutch your hands,
Tottering legs that follow you everywhere,

To,
Wandering souls,
Expressive minds

Your tiny tot
To be a grown person

There are times,
When days stretch,
Hours cease to end

But like all things,
Good and bad,
They come to an end

And one day,
You will be lost in thoughts,
In old pictures,
In memories

When you were still needed,
When you were still their 'No.1'

And you will realize,
Those calls and meetings could have been prolonged,
Those 'time out' sessions weren't really necessary,

That extra five minutes of TV time,
Those nights when they refused to sleep without you,
That tiny hand holding yours

Well, that is what mattered,
That is the only thing and person who will matter

And I will go on to say,
It matters more than yourself

Because, you can get your career, friends and social
life back
But
The child once lost in adulthood
Is something you are never getting back.

My Daughter, My Parent

You smile at me,
When I am at my lowest

You lift me up,
When there's nothing to cheer

You call me 'yours' with pride,
When I am a mess

You challenge me,
When I am supposed to be the one teaching you

You see,
I might be your parent

But most times,
You are the one parenting me

You never know,
When it's the last time

You are so busy complaining and comparing,
competing and struggling to keep with the
monotony

That, you don't realise that this could be the LAST

It could be the last time,
Your child asks you to comb their hair,
Your child asks you to read her a bedtime story or
two,
Your child asks you to help her shower and dress
up,

Because,
As the days go by,
Your child doesn't remain as little, anymore.

While, we pray and hope they grow up soon,
We forget, that they will,
They will grow up

And never be so little ever again.

This is a reminder, to you and to me,
To us all,
Pick them up one more time
Hug them tight,
Shower them and change their clothes,
Comb their hair and dress them up,
Play dolls and cars with them,
Go the extra mile,

Because, it's all worth it
As, once they grow up,
They will never be so little again.

What if it's the last time?

The day you become a parent,
Your life changes

From the day, your child is born
You are not the same anymore

Sure, you can say,
That you will not give up on your freedom or
independence,
You will remain the same woman that you were
but the truth is,
You will not!

From the time your child is born,
the second you wake up to the last seconds before
you fall asleep
will go in thinking about your child

Nothing you do will ever feel enough,
You will second-guess all your actions and thoughts

But instead of trying to be the best and
second-guessing everything,

How about we just embrace the rest?

Let's embrace the long nights and longer days,
the messy homes and messier hair,
the umpteen pretend plays and hours of nursery
rhymes,

Because,
You never know when it will be the last,
the last time you will hear that nursery rhyme,
the last time they hold your hand and hug you tight
on reaching the school gate,
the dependency on you for every single thing

It could be the last time
And,
You will never know that this is the last time
Until,
You never do it again.

You are Enough

My dear girl,

How I want to protect you,

I want to shelter you,

Keep you warm,

Keep you safe,

I want to steer you away from the bad,

I want to steer you away from the evil,

But I cannot,

How can I expect you to learn,

If I don't give you the opportunity?

How can I expect you to rise to your potential,

If I don't let you stumble on your mistakes and
rise?

My little girl,

I want you to always remember,

The world is not a good one,

There's too much hatred,

There's a lot of competition,

You will come across a lot of people,

Who will resent you,

Who will compete with you,

Who will take credit for your work,

Who will do anything to sabotage you

And,

Those times will be tough,

You will want to quit,

You will want to give up

But remember,

My little girl,

Even when you won't be so little,

There is goodness in this world too,

There is peace,

There is faith,

There is appreciation

And there are people,

Who believe you,

Who need you,

Who want you,

And who love you, endlessly, selflessly and timelessly

If there's one thing I wish for you to remember,

It will be this—

You are enough,

You are your biggest competition,

Your strengths,

Your personality,

Your sincerity,

YOU

You will shine through

And,

Never let anyone,

Make you second-guess yourself.

You are Enough!

Be Strong, My Girl

I can only pray,

I make you strong

To fight the tidal waves,

To overcome the shadows in the dark,

To conquer the highest of mountains

My darling girl,

I don't want to parent you,

I want to raise you,

I want to make you able,

To face any hurdle on the way

And as much as I want to shelter you,

I know, that's not the way

I can't and don't want to keep you caged

You, my bluebird with a nightingale's voice

Belong in the sky,

Soaring high above the clouds

I will always be right behind you.

Protecting you,

Pampering you,

Cheering you

Because my darling,

You are loved much more than you know

And, you deserve it all!

Changes

"Some days are easy,

Some days are hard,

But all days,

Are equally humbling,

Reminding you:

How you help your little one everyday,

And,

How your little one changes your perspective on life every single day..."

My Baby Girl, You shall always
be..

Even as a baby,

You had a mind of your own

And I let you show the way

As I held your hand

Tiny to small,

In the blink of an eye,

You kept on growing

Until I saw you

And, you were no longer

The gap-toothed toddler running to hold me

You were reaching my shoulders

Standing tall

And looking confident and proud

As you walked alongside me

Tears came to my eyes,

As I reminisced about the years that flew by

But

They were tears of joy

Because big or small,

No matter how old you get

My little girl,

The baby I cradled in my arms,

The tiny hands that pulled me to places,

The tight hugs that completed and still complete my day,

The 'invisible' dimpled smile that lit up any corner,

My baby girl, you shall always be..

I am your Mom

In your highs,

In your lows,

In your brightest days,

In your saddest times,

I will be there

You don't need to ask,

You don't need to explain,

You don't even need to acknowledge.

You just need to say, "Mom…"

And, your tone will say it all to me

Because

I am your biggest protector

I am your biggest fan,

I will raise you up

And, I will always help you get up when you fall

I will love you unconditionally,

From zero to infinity

I don't need a Mother's Day card

Or extravagant gifts professing your love for me

Let me be your call,

The call, when you are in trouble,

The call, when you are feeling low,

The call, when you are alone

Let me be your go-to person forever

Because,

No matter who stays,

And who leaves

You shall always have me,

Your mom, who loves you unconditionally

Who's growing so fine?

I see you grow,

Oh, so fine.

From singing nursery rhymes

To becoming a Swiftie,

You have grown,

In the blink of an eye

Where did those years go, I wonder?

Did you grow up when we were sleeping each
night?

How did the little girl who I cradled to sleep each
night,

Become an independent person with a mind and
personality of her own?

When did you become so big,

Helping me cook in the kitchen,

Folding your own blankets,

Deciding your own outfits,

When did the open door,
Start getting shut?

Why is your growth,

My biggest pride

But, also a stark reminder

Of how time flies

My girl,

Who's growing so fine,

Yesterday, today and forever,

I am just grateful,

I can call you mine.

Sometimes..

Sometimes I say a lot,

Sometimes I say nothing at all,

There are times,

When we have a bad day,

When we bicker over everything

But,

Not a single day in life

Have I ever regretted you

How could I possibly describe what you mean to
me?

How could I describe the star that you are to me?

You are the brightest star in any sky

You are the rainbow on a cloudy day

Don't second-guess my anger,

Don't second-guess my thoughts for you,

I could be in a bad mood,

I could even get angry at you,

But

Never will I stop loving you,

And

I will always be thankful

That I am yours

And

You are mine!

Be happy with being YOU!

I want my daughter

To know herself

To know her strength

To know her weakness

To love fiercely

To live independently

I want my daughter

To know that when someone says she looks good,

It's for more than her looks

I want her to be pretty

but

I don't want her to be shallow

I want her to read a lot

but

I want her to live a lot more

I want her to take bold risks,

I want her to make calculated decisions,

I want her to learn to stand up for herself,

Some may push her,

Some may dissuade her decisions

But

I want her to know

She should always stick up for herself

Because,

One day, long after I am gone

One day, when she's all grown up and a mom of her own

If nothing more,

She should know,

My mom taught me to be happy with myself!

Imperfectly Perfect

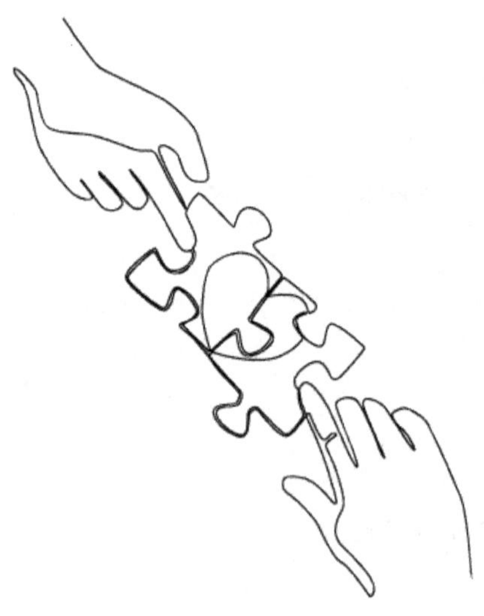

Your mumma is not perfect,

She comes with a lot of faults,

She comes with a lot of weaknesses,

A lot of mood swings and temper issues,

Your mumma doesn't know how to make round
rotis,

She is a fussy eater,

She doesn't like to experiment,

She despises change

Your mumma is not perfect in many things,

But despite her imperfections and faults,

If there is one thing she can say for certain,

Is she loves you endlessly,

She loves you infinitely

And, despite my imperfections,

The girl you are growing up to be

reflects

that if nothing else,

Motherhood is one thing I have excelled in!

Always A Little Girl

I brush my mother's worries aside,

At times, I lose my cool with her,

More than once,

I am restless and impatient with her

I come home,

I try to brush your wildly flying hair,

You brush my hands away,

Impatiently and restlessly,

"Mumma, it's fine.."

I see you get impatient,

I see you get restless,

I see you

And,

I see myself

You see, my little girl

I am my mother's little girl too

I might be your mumma

But your beloved grandma is my mumma too

I realize then,

Not much has changed with the generations and time,

Because a mother's love is eternal,

And, a mother can never undo the sight of you as a little girl,

For her,

You will always be her baby girl

And,

Long after you become a mother

And your mini-me gives you exasperated looks and answers,

You will brush it all aside,

Because,

You will always be a little girl.

A prayer for my daughter

A prayer for my daughter,

A solemn wish I always make,

May you take each step with pride,

Take each step with faith in your abilities,

And, confidence in your mind

May you defy the odds,

And,

Work beyond materialistic pursuits

A prayer for my daughter,

A solemn wish I always make,

May you be proud of who you are,

But, never be arrogant

May you always look and feel good,

But, never judge another person based on what they
wear and how they look

A prayer for my daughter,

A solemn wish I always make,

May you always put in your best,

And never give in, never give up

May you always remember

That no matter what your age is,

No matter which part of the world you are,

You will always have me,

Someone to fall back on,

Someone to trust,

Someone who infinitely loves and believes you,

Because for the world,

You may be just another girl,

But for me,

You are my world!

Hand In Hand

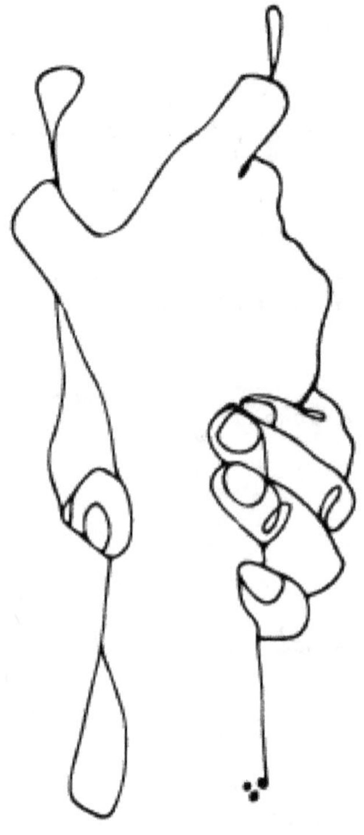

I was a bit scared,

I was terrified,

Here you came,

So tiny,

So innocent,

So beautiful

And,

Oh, so vulnerable

Nobody really tells you,

How hard it gets,

How vulnerable babies are

And, how much on you they depend

You must understand,

I was a bit of a baby, myself,

Grown-up in age,

But, a child very much at heart

I was so scared,

I was so terrified,

How was I supposed to take care of you,

When honestly, I have barely taken care of myself

But then, you saw me with your big beautiful eyes,

You saw right through me,

And held on to me tight

As if telling me,

"Don't worry, Mother. I am there with you,

And, together we both will get through."

Now, at nine and growing up so fine,

I can't ever believe there was a time,

When I doubted how I would love and care for you,
my child

You see, my dear girl,

I might have made you

But you made me the woman and mother I am today

And, we both raised each other, holding hands,

Weathering storms,

Emerging together absolutely fine.

One day..

One day, you'll want to know how I came to be so strong,

You'll want to know how I managed to do everything I did,

You'll want to know how I functioned with four hours of sleep,

You'll want to know how I came up with recipes having sneaky broccolis and zucchinis,

You'll want to know how I spent hours playing with dolls and watching cartoons that I outgrew decades ago,

You'll want to know where I got the confidence from, to speak out when it's wrong, to fight for your voice,

You'll want to know how to be a full-time mother while still being a daughter, a sister, a friend, a wife and a woman,

You'll want to know how I managed to do all this
and more without ever making you feel inadequate,
unloved or insufficient in this big, bad world

I will tell you, then, what my mother told me and
her mother told her,

"Become a mother and you'll know…"

Wild Child

You are the wild child,

You break the stereotypes,

You ask a question for every action,

You think and talk your mind

In this world of rules and boundaries,

You yearn to break free,

You have a voice that's strong,

That you are not afraid to use,

You are the wild child,

You are labelled naughty,

You are called a brat,

You are mischievous,

You are boisterous,

You are the rebel,

The odd one amongst the similes

Not everyone understands you,

Not everybody likes you,

But, my child,

I want you to be wild,

I want you, your big eyes and your bigger mind to
see and be the change

For today,

You may be labelled as rebellious and wild,

And tomorrow,

The same people will say your name wistfully,

For, she may be wild

But at least,

She dared to do something more,

She dared to go the extra mile

And, she lived.

All I see is YOU...

Baby Girl,

All I see is you,

My eyes are a bit weary,

My mind is a bit overwhelmed

But

Don't you fret, my child

All I see is you

When you feel,

The doors are closing in,

The days are getting longer,

When you can't see beyond here and now,

Remember,

I am here

And,

All I see is you

When you think,

You have achieved nothing,

When all you see is failure,

Remember my words,

You are my biggest achievement,

You are my pride,

You are my joy,

And, no matter what you think you can or cannot
do,

What you achieved or did,

You are what matters,

You are the one I will choose, over and over

Nights are long,

Days are longer,

Nothing and everything matters

Because

You are You

And

All I see is you.

More than your pretty face

She is so cute, they say.
She is strong too, I retort back.

She has such a flexible body, they say.
She has a strong mind too, I retort back.

She is so kind and caring, they say.
She is generous and street smart too, I retort back.

This world is always going to define you within
labels.

The world yearns for names,

But these words are just adjectives,

They don't say who you are

There are no words to describe

The way you look when you are sleeping clutching
your soft toy,

The kindness you show to a poor person,

The ease with which you part your toys for someone
needy,

You are far more than your pretty face,

You are far beyond anybody's expectation

And,

You are not everybody's cup of tea

That's good, my girl

Because, you are not just everybody either.

Like a Rose...

You are but a rosebud,

Small, pink, wiggly,

Growing a little everyday,

Blooming a little every time I see you,

And,

Before I know,

You will become a Rose,

Lovely and strong,

Delicate and beautiful,

But with thorns,

A roughness not everyone can handle

There are many flowers,

Blooming in the field, my dear

Each one more delicate,

More beautiful than the last one

But,

There's nothing like a rose,

Soft and fragrant,

And edges so rough,

You are bound to get hurt if you don't handle with care

Be delicate yet strong,

Be bold yet with rough edges,

Be confident in your skin,

Bloom without a fear in the world,

Soar high in the sky

Because,

There is no flower as beautiful as a rose,

There is no person as unique as you.

When being a Mumma was
everything..

It's just 5 am,

The sun is still not yet out

But

It is time to start your day

Before you even have a cup of coffee,

You hear tiny footsteps climbing down the stairs,

Lunchbox to make,

Breakfasts to fill a little tummy,

Appointments to make and keep,

Amidst the cuddles and boo-boos,

It's afternoon,

And, you realize

You still haven't had your cup of coffee

You sit down,

Take in what's around you,

The house is a mess,

Your hair is a spider's web,

Your face looks like it has never been washed

And

Your YouTube history doesn't cater to anyone
grown-up,

You look at your phone,

It's a go yet again

The days are exhausting and long,

You wish for things to remain the same

Yet hurry up

Later,

The days will remain long

But

You won't complain

The tiny footsteps that you yearn to hear,

Will grow and have their doors closed to you,

The boo-boos that you yearn to kiss,

Will grow into a person beyond your shoulder,

You finally have time to do your hair,

Your coffee is no longer drunk cold,

There are no toys waiting to be picked up in every corner,

You grew up,

But

Instead of feeling free

I long for the days,

When my days and nights were relentless,

Yet my heart was filled to the brim

There was a time,

Not that long ago,

You only needed me

And

I only had time for you

We were chaotic and crazy,

Messy and exhausted

But

Now,

I wished I had slowed down

I craved for space without you,

I craved to get an identity for myself,

I craved to find my 'me time'

Now,

I have it all,

But

I just want to hear

"Mumma" being called from upstairs again,

Tiny footsteps, running through the house,

Lego pieces that used to be everywhere

And

I will abandon it all,

Because,

I realize now,

You needing me is all I need

To be ME.

Will you remember...?

Will you remember,

Way back ago,

When I rocked and held you,

When I whispered sweet nothing to your ears,

And

You heard my voice,

Sighed in contentment

And slept

Will you remember,

Your first birthday

Where both your grandparents were there,

We took a gazillion photos,

You said NO to cake,

Had your milk,

Hugged me tight and slept

Will you remember,

Your first day of school,

I cried along with you,

Waited for hours outside the gate,

Till I saw you, held you

And hugged you tight

Will you remember,

When you would get nightmares every other night,

You saw a flying tiger,

Sometimes, a flock of deer

And

I would open the blinds while you held on to me
tight,

"You are safe, my love..." I would whisper in your
ears

You refused to let go of me for hours

And clung tighter every time I tried to leave

Will you remember,

So many memories like these,

The biggest of all,

When I saw you for the first time

And

Dedicated to you, my heart and life

One day,

As you get bigger and older,

When you have children of your own,

I will see you,
Hold them tight
And

Whisper sweet nothings in their ears

You will catch my eye

And ask me,

"Mumma, will they remember all this...?"

I won't say a word,

I will smile,

I would have got my answer

As I hear you whisper,

"I love you" as I am closing the door.

I didn't Wish For You..

As the stars shone bright in the endless sky,

I looked up at them

And

I looked at the tiny hand clutching mine

How did I get this far?

I didn't wish for you upon a shooting star

I didn't pray and cry for you to be mine

I lived my life,

I laughed,

I travelled

And

I enjoyed

You came along,

Suddenly and unexpectedly

I know I didn't wish for you

I was not even sure if I could care for you

But

You gazed deep into my eyes,

You held my pinky finger with your tiny hand

When I saw that night upon the starry sky

I closed my eyes

And made one wish,

Made my first wish, in fact

Whichever star brought you to me,

I, thank you

I may not have wished,

I may not have asked

But

Today

I see you beside me

And

I know

The wish I didn't even know I had came true.

Imperfectly Perfect

Underweight and tiny,

Smaller than I had ever seen anybody,

You cried louder than the lion's roar in the jungle,

Your face wrinkled with tears,

I was not scared,

I was terrified

How could I be your mother,

If I couldn't understand you?

How could I hug and comfort you,

When I was afraid to hold you?

I cried a lot of nights,

I shook my head from left to right,

I couldn't possibly be able to take care of you,

I couldn't possibly be able to raise you right

I wanted to quit

Even though, I knew I couldn't

But then something miraculous happened,

Amidst the tears and fears,

I realized, I had learned to hold you right

I learnt to wipe your tears

And, kiss away your fears

When on the days,

It got so overwhelming,

I couldn't sleep and eat right,

I looked at you,

The creation that created a new me

And

I know

As long as we are together,

We will both be alright.

Don't Listen

Go deep in the jungle,

Go deeper in the sea,

Soar high above the trampoline can take you,

Climb every thorny tree

Don't listen to me, I tell you

Don't listen to my fears and abide,

As a mother,

I am bound to worry,

That's what I am,

Being a worrier is a part of my job

Shout louder than the others,

Sing the tune of life,

There will always be

Someone who says NO

And

I am telling you

Don't listen,

Just let loose

Don't listen to me, my baby

Don't listen to my fears and sighs,

I will always be afraid for you,

I will never want to let you go

But

You are a storm,

A gust of wind on a hot day

And

It is your job

To fly and soar beyond the imaginable,

As I see you go...

Thoughts

There are times I gaze outside the window,

You ask, "Mumma, what do you keep looking for
outside?"

How do I tell you,

What am I looking at,

I might be gazing outside

But my thoughts are far beyond the scenery outside

I am looking at the trees,

And picturing you as a toddler,

Running around the park

I am looking at the blue sky,

And envisioning you in your first blue jumper,

When you were toothless and grinned at me

I am looking at the cyclists on the road,

And see you in your pink helmet,

Falling and getting up on the bumpy roads with
ease

There are times, my child

When I might be looking outside

But my thoughts are lost far behind,

Of times that passed by

And times that are yet to come

But, never does a moment pass,

When I don't think of you.

End Point

Let me be your End point,

Let me be your Plan of Action,

Let me be your plan A and B,

I will draw a map of the world,

On the back of your hands

And, each time you fall,

Every time you fail,

You will look at the map

And,

Find your way back to your end point,

I cannot protect you from falls and fails,

I cannot shelter you from storms and hails,

I cannot be everywhere with you,

You will grow soon,

Move beyond tiaras and realize that real
superheroes don't wear capes,

You will grow up,

Finding that not everyone who befriends you wants
to be your friend

You will grow up,

Finding out that there will be two or at the most,
three who would fight for and not with you

Look at the map,

The world is in your hands,

Your destiny is in your palms

And,

Remember at every end point,

You will find me there.